LAZY LAMA LOOKS AT

Living without fear and anger

RINGU TULKU RINPOCHE

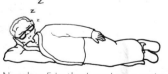

Number 5 in the Lazy Lama series

Bodhicharya
PUBLICATIONS

Awaken the heart by opening the mind

First Published in 2005 by
BODHICHARYA PUBLICATIONS
24 Chester Street, Oxford, OX4 1SN, United Kingdom.
www.bodhicharya.org   email: publications@bodhicharya.com

ISBN 0 9534489 4 0
Second Edition. 2013.

First transcribed by Brigit Habetz.
Edited by Andy Powers 2005.

Typesetting & Design by Paul O'Connor at Judo Design, Ireland.

Printed on recycled paper by Imprint Digital, Devon, UK.

Cover Image: ©Paul O'Connor.
Internal illustrations: Andy Powers
Lazy Lama logo: Dr Conrad Harvey & Rebecca O'Connor

Editor's Preface

This is the fifth booklet in the uniquely relaxed Lazy Lama series. It is based on a talk given by Ringu Tulku Rinpoché at Kagyu Benchen Ling in Freiburg, Germany, 1998, at the invitation of Chime Rinpoché and his students.

We would like to thank Ringu Tulku himself for the simple but profound wisdom contained in this booklet. It is wisdom that is much yearned for and much needed in our world at this time.

Andy Powers
2005

Living without fear and anger

People often ask me how Buddhist teachings can help them in their day-to-day lives. What is there in the ancient teachings of the Buddha that can be of relevance to our modern world? The Buddha taught how it is possible to find peace and happiness despite the many problems we face in our lives, and, in particular, how we can deal with our negative emotions. In Buddhist scriptures these are sometimes described as mind-poisons, because they can poison our whole outlook on life. How can we stop this from happening?

In this small booklet, I will discuss ways in which we can learn to deal with two of the most destructive mind-poisons, ones which are very closely linked with each other: fear and anger. To begin with let's look at anger and what we can do when we get angry.

Fighting injustice and anger

Many people believe that anger isn't always negative and that, in certain circumstances, it is actually good to be angry. I've had many debates over the years with people who say that without anger we wouldn't have the energy to fight injustice, and it's sometimes difficult to argue that this view is completely wrong. However, from the Buddhist perspective, being angry is never positive, because when we are taken over by anger we lose our self-control and our capacity to make well-judged decisions. Not only that, but most of the time our own anger actually hurts us. Being angry isn't a nice experience: nobody likes to be angry. Nobody says: "Oh, this morning I had such a nice time, I was so angry!"

When we are angry we suffer. Of course, whomever we are angry with will not be having the best time either, and this is sometimes the main reason for our anger: we want to make

that person feel as uncomfortable as possible. However, it is not just that person who will suffer. We and everybody around us will be affected as well. It is really tough to be in the vicinity of somebody who is very angry. The whole of the surrounding area seems to be charged with their negative energy. Something that makes us miserable and makes everybody around us miserable cannot be a good thing.

But what can we do when we become angry because we see, hear, or read about the terrible things happening in the world? Shouldn't we feel angry then? In these circumstances we have to ask ourselves if our anger is really helpful. If we want to do something good when we see something bad, something unjust, it is best not to react with anger. When we are angry our minds do not behave reasonably, or logically, because our thoughts are being driven by intense emotion. When we are not thinking reasonably or logically it is easy for us to end up adding to the hate and anger that

caused the unjust situation in the first place. Therefore, anger is not useful in the face of injustice. Is there another way of reacting?

Buddhist teachings tell us that in every situation in which it is possible to react with anger, it is also possible to respond with compassion. When we see something happening which is not good, which is not nice, which is not just, we can either become angry or we can become compassionate. How can compassion and anger arise from the same situation? We get angry when our mind is focused solely upon blaming an individual, or a group of people, and attacking them for a particular state of affairs: "This person is very, very bad! It is all his fault!" If instead we focus on the situation itself, and its causes, then it is said compassion can arise, because we are not merely attacking somebody, but trying to solve the problem. If we are thinking about what can be done, rather than looking for someone to blame, then our focus is on trying to change things for the better, not

just on hitting out at someone.

The energy generated by responding to difficult situations with compassion has a much longer life than that created by anger. Anger grows like a flame and burns out like a flame. It is true that when the flame of anger is burning within us the intense energy we feel can drive us to do all sorts of things, but a lot of what we might do in this state of mind may make bad situations worse. On the other hand, if our actions are inspired by compassion, then our energy will be sustained much longer: until the situation has been genuinely put right. Therefore, it is much more useful for us to fight injustice by becoming compassionate than by becoming angry.

Anger is useless

I think it is very important to understand deeply that to be angry, to bear a grudge, to keep hatred and bad feelings inside us is completely useless.

It is neither good for us nor for anybody else. It's very important that we really appreciate this right from the first moment we start trying to work on our emotions.

Why do we get angry in the first place? We get angry because somebody does something unpleasant to us. This is somewhat ironic, because, as I've already said, being angry is far from pleasant, so by getting angry we are doing our enemy's job for them: we're helping them hurt us. We don't feel any happier when we are angry, we feel unhappy and tense. Therefore, we don't have to think of it from someone else's point of view: "I should not get angry because it's bad for this person." The main point is that I am not going to get angry, I am not going to bear a grudge, and I am not going to become hateful, because that's not good for me. It's not good for others either, but first and foremost it's not good for me. Whether our anger will hurt the person whom we are angry with is not certain. Maybe it will hurt

them, maybe it will not. But it is absolutely certain that our anger will hurt us. As long as we are angry we suffer. Learning how to let go of our hatred and rage is, therefore, a way of defeating our enemy. When we look at it this way, it is much easier to work on our anger.

Compassion is light

Sometimes people I meet tell me that they feel worn down by trying to be compassionate and nice. They say: "I have tried to be so very patient and compassionate, but I can't take it anymore!" They feel really bad and weighed down because they feel unable to live up to being the kind of person they think they should be. This is due to a misunderstanding of compassion. When we are trying to work on our anger and trying to be more compassionate, it's not that we are doing a favour for someone. We are doing it for our own good, because we don't want to suffer and being angry will make us suffer. It's as simple as that! If

7

we don't understand this we may well associate trying to be compassionate with a feeling of being burdened, but compassion itself is actually a very light and joyful emotion. Being angry, on the other hand, definitely does weigh us down, because it's always associated with something unpleasant. When we keep something inside us that is unpleasant, it will quite naturally cause us suffering. Compassion is nothing like that. Compassion is general goodwill. It's just wishing good. It's not necessarily taking up the responsibility of helping everybody; you can't help everybody. Nobody can help everybody, but we can wish everybody well, and if there is a chance for us to do something good, that's even better.

Perhaps it is worth pointing out here, that being compassionate – having benevolent wishes for others – does not depend upon our liking everyone. We don't need to like someone to wish them well. There are good and not so good people in the world, people

we like to be with, and people we would rather not spend our time with. But why should we have ill feelings towards anyone? If we don't like someone we can avoid them, or try our best to just get along with them. There is no need to wish someone ill. If we do we will end up poisoning our own enjoyment of life.

I have often had people come to me and say that they feel unable to express their true feelings because they have been brought up to be 'nice' and they now feel they have to repress all their anger. They say: "My parents made me nice and compassionate, so I can't really express myself." Repressing our feelings is not what we are trying to do here, because if we do that we are still being angry, we're just not showing it. When the teachings say: "Try not to be angry", they don't mean push your anger down inside yourself and then try to stick a smile on your face. That's not useful to anyone. They are talking about not being angry at all, not simply hiding our anger.

From time to time we will become angry, and a little bit of anger, for example, losing our temper a bit, isn't really too much of a problem and we shouldn't feel too bad about ourselves because of that. Some people seem to be naturally a little bit short tempered. I think that's acceptable, it's okay, it's just the way some people are. After a while people come to know what they're like, so it's not too serious and they don't cause too much harm to others or themselves. Of course, if we lose our temper all the time, we will be constantly doing and saying things that we will regret later. But the most important thing to remember is that we should not hold on to our anger. When we start to bear grudges – when our anger is something that we don't let go of – this is when it's a real problem. The more we keep anger inside us, the heavier we will feel. Likewise, the more we can learn to genuinely let go of our anger, the lighter we will feel.

When we understand deeply that being angry and keeping anger and hatred inside us, is totally useless – it doesn't benefit us, it doesn't benefit anybody else – then we can start to work on it. If we don't appreciate this,

11

then working on our anger might feel more like we are 'not allowed' to be angry, and we might think: "I am a Buddhist, therefore I am not allowed to be angry." This isn't the right attitude, because if I am 'not allowed to be angry' then the first time something happens that makes me angry, perhaps someone isn't very nice to me or ignores me, then I say to myself: "Okay, he isn't a nice person, but I am a Buddhist! I am not allowed to be angry. I must forgive him." The second time he does something that I don't like I say to myself: "He really isn't a nice person at all! But I am a Buddhist!! I am not allowed to be angry!" And then the third time I've had enough and think: "Buddhist my foot, I am really angry!!!"

It's not because I am a Buddhist or because I am a Christian that I should not get angry. It's simply that being angry is not good for anybody. Keeping anger inside us in particular, is misery for others and misery for ourselves. It's of no use. It's absolutely useless. It's not

beneficial in any way. It's a bad habit, and like every bad habit we should try slowly to work on it, with the understanding that it is harmful to us. If we do that, then it will gradually become less of a habit and we can eventually replace it with a more positive way of dealing with whatever situation we are in.

Hurt and hate

The primary cause of harbouring anger and resentment inside us is the feeling of hurt. I feel hurt, therefore I feel angry, and I feel resentful. If somebody does something nasty to us, then we feel hurt, especially if that person is someone we care about. When that happens we feel extremely hurt, and if we keep this feeling of hurt inside us it can eventually turn into hatred. This is something we really need to work on.

I think we need to appreciate that it is really not that unusual for people to act badly.

Most people, including ourselves, are under the influence of negative emotions, whether it is anger, greed, or whatever, so if somebody hurts us it's not that surprising or out of the ordinary. If people are under the control of negative emotions then they will do crazy things. When people are totally overcome by these emotions, they even consciously hurt themselves. If someone is in a state of mind where they can wilfully hurt themselves, why should hurting someone else seem like a big deal to them? When someone says something to us, or does something that is totally negative, that person is in bad shape and in a deeply unhappy state of mind. Okay, they did something to us, something bad, perhaps terrible, but the longer we keep hold of that feeling of hurt and anger, the worse it is for us. If we can train ourselves to look at these situations from this point of view then we can eventually say: "Okay, it was not a good thing that person did. It was very painful, but it's finished now and I want to let

it go. I don't want to cling onto it any more. I don't want to keep it any more." We can do this in just the same way that we don't keep hold of the negative things that happened to us in our dreams. Sometimes we have very bad dreams, but in the morning we don't feel too bad and can soon shrug off the emotion, because we know that it was only a dream, even though it all seemed very real when we were dreaming. The past is a little bit like a dream – it's gone, it doesn't come back, it's only in our memory – so I think we should try to treat difficult times like a dream. They hurt, they were bad, they were painful, but we can't change whatever happened, so we don't want to keep hold of that feeling of hurt, because that will harm us even more. The sooner we can let go of the hurt, the better it is. Of course, we still have the memory, but we don't need to keep the hatred. I think that is possible. That is definitely possible and that is the training in Buddhist practice.

In Tibet, when the Chinese chased us, we

had lots of nightmares. But I do not believe that we should hate the Chinese, because the people who were attacking us were not free. In a way nobody is free, because everyone is, to some extent, a prisoner of his or her negative emotions. Therefore, although the memory remains, we can still have peace in our minds, because our hearts are free of hatred.

Facing our fears

Anger and hatred are very much related to fear. In fact, I believe that fear is the basis of all negative emotions. Dealing with fear is not an easy thing to do. Some people think: "I am brave. I don't have any fear. I can do bungee-jumping!" But our fundamental fear is subtle and deep-seated, and it is on the basis of this fear that all kinds of negative emotions arise. There are many different meditations and practices to help us deal with our fear, but the basic thing we have to do is to learn how

to face it. We try to look our fear in the face. It's not an easy thing to do; it is not easy to let go of anger either. However, little by little we can work on our emotions, through study, reflection, and meditation, until eventually we can totally rid ourselves of our negative emotions. We can be free of anger and fear, and we can be truly happy and content. We have to develop confidence in ourselves and believe that we can do this.

In a famous Buddhist teaching, the Bodhicharyavatara, it is stated:

> *If you can change something there is no*
> *need to be unhappy about it.*
> *If you cannot change it, there is no use*
> *being unhappy about it.*

I think this stanza is very important. We need to be able to look at a situation and say: "What can I do? Can I do something to improve this?" If we can do something to

improve things – to relieve pain and suffering – okay. Let's go and do that. There is no need to be angry. There is no need to panic. There is no need to be worried. If we can't do anything to improve a bad situation, then being angry about it, panicking, or worrying is of no use! All we can do is prepare for the worst.

What is the worst that can happen? When we look at it, most of the time the worst is not that bad. Many times we make things more dramatic in our minds than they actually are. Our imagination is very powerful. If we want to make something nice, we make it out to be much nicer than it actually is, and if we want to make something dreadful, we make it out to be much, much more terrible than it actually is. But if we can look at things realistically, most of the time they are not that bad. Even if the worst really is going to happen and maybe we are going to die, everybody has to die one day, some sooner, some later. So, if it is to be now then that's okay, that's the way it is. There

is a saying: A brave man dies once in his life
and a coward dies a hundred times. Panicking
is useless! It is a waste of our life. When we are
prepared for the worst, our fear is a little less,
and we are less easily hurt. If we feel less hurt,
we will harbour less anger and resentment.

Exercising understanding

This understanding of anger and fear is very important. However, 'an understanding' is not enough. Sometimes people believe that if we understand something like this intellectually then that's enough, but that is not the case. If our understanding remains theoretical, then it won't help us when we are faced with an actual problem. Abstract understanding will not change our life; it will not change our experience. We need to change our experience, change our habits and our conditioning by exercising our understanding: reminding ourselves again and again, and trying to apply it to our daily life. We won't be able to deal with very big problems to begin with, but we will be capable of using our understanding to help us with small problems. If we learn how to apply our understanding to very little things, then when somebody says

something that hurts us, we can remember the understanding and say: "Okay, today he's not very happy. He must have had a fight with his wife this morning or something like that. He is not being himself." And then we don't take things so personally or hold on to the problem. When we are used to that sort of situation, then slowly but surely we can begin to deal with the bigger problems in life too. That's what Buddhist practice is: reminding ourselves again and again that emotions like hatred and fear are useless, and being mindful of how we react to things.

Sometimes all we need is a little bit of mindfulness, because if we have an understanding of something, then our mindfulness will bring that understanding home.

Meditation

Meditation is a way of going deeper into ourselves, and it allows us to reach a more

subtle level of understanding. We have to familiarise ourselves with our understanding of emotions until it becomes part of us. It is sometimes described as the longest journey: the journey from the head to the heart. First we have to calm the mind, so we start by sitting and trying to be a bit more restful, relaxed and at peace. It is important, therefore, that, before we begin the meditation, we try to arrange our time so that we won't be disturbed, even if all we can manage is five minutes.

Sitting properly is a way of releasing tension and if we can sit in the traditional lotus position that's very good, though it's not completely necessary. The main thing is to be comfortable, but with your back straight and your body not leaning to either side or forwards or backwards. Check for any tension in the body, and the face too. The face should feel soft and relaxed, the teeth not grinding or clenched, and the lips slightly open and relaxed. The eyes can be slightly open or gently

closed. A balanced and relaxed posture is the starting point. Just sit for a little while and enjoy that relaxed feeling and do nothing else but enjoy it.

Now we need to look at the mind. It would be nice if we could relax the mind as easily as the body, but it's usually not that easy. In Buddhist teachings the mind is often described as being like a monkey jumping from tree to tree. When we first sit quietly in meditation it appears that the mind is even more monkey-like than usual. This is only because we are more aware of the mind and can see how much it jumps about from one problem to another or one fantasy to another. It seems that we can't stop the mind: the more we try to control it, the more it runs around uncontrollably. All we can do is let thoughts and emotions come and go and this is actually the key to meditation. We do not try to do anything with our thoughts, we let them come up and let them go: we just let be. We don't

become entangled with our thoughts or judge whether one thought is good and another bad. It is sometimes described as being like an old person in a park watching children play. This old person can enjoy watching whatever drama unfolds, but he or she doesn't become involved, because it is only children playing. During meditation thoughts come and go, emotions come and go; we don't react, we do nothing, we just relax and let be.

When we begin meditating this is really all we have to do. After a while we will start to realise that by just letting be, our emotions and thoughts will just come and go, and we will no longer be overwhelmed by them. Once we have learned this, we will gain the confidence that we are actually in control of our emotions. They do not have control over us.

Through meditation, our mind will slowly become more spacious and aware, and we will become angry less often. When we do become angry we will be aware that it is not something

we have to hold on to. There is no reason to hold on to such things. Our thoughts and emotions, both good and bad, come and go. They are all fleeting. This is understanding with awareness.

Discussion

Questioner: When I get angry it's as though I'm taken over, and it's too late to do anything about it. Is there a way to train myself to recognize the precursors of anger, so that I can deal with it before it actually arises and becomes too much?

Rinpoche: We need to train ourselves to be vigilant and aware. As I said earlier, anger is always associated with something unpleasant. Therefore, when something really unpleasant happens to us, we can predict that we are going to get angry. At that point, reminding ourselves of the useless nature of anger can be helpful. When it goes beyond that point, when we can feel anger rushing around inside us, and feel driven to do something which we know is not good, then it is best to do as the Indian saint Shantideva advises: "Become like a log." Don't say anything, don't do

anything, and don't react. Most of the time, if we don't react straight away – if we delay our reaction for even a few seconds – then our reaction will be different. We would not say what we were going to say. We would not do what we were going to do. If we feel like smashing a cup we say: "Okay, I will smash it, but in thirty seconds time." Then we wait for thirty seconds and see whether we really want to smash it. Maybe we won't feel like smashing it – after all we'd have to buy a new one! I think postponing our actions is a very practical way of dealing with our anger. If we don't react straight away, then the bursting energy of anger cools down a little bit, just enough to let us think through our actions.

If you are a good meditator, then instead of taking this approach, you can actually learn to transform your anger. Sometimes it is recommended that when our anger arises, we just look into the anger and relax. If we see the true nature of this anger – that

actually there's nothing there to get caught up in or cling to – then we can turn it into wisdom. Instead of following the surge of our thoughts, we look directly at our feelings and relax into them. We don't try to stop anything, or repress anything – we just relax into the feeling. When we have learned how to do this it is a very effective method for dealing with our emotions. Mastering this technique doesn't mean we will never have anger again, but it does mean that we will be able to deal with our anger when it arises. All the work we do with our emotions has to happen in this way: we can only ever work on our anger and fear on a momentto-moment basis. However, if we can learn how to deal with our anger in this moment, then we'll be able to work on it in the next moment. After a while we will develop confidence in our ability to deal with these emotions. Then it will become a habit.

Our personality is basically a collection

of habits -some good, some not so good. If we develop a habit of doing something even for a short time it is very difficult to change it. A bad habit like smoking is very hard to break, even if we have not been a smoker for very long. Breaking bad habits that have established themselves over a long period is even harder, but from the Buddhist point of view it is possible. And it is possible to develop new and positive habits.

It is said in Buddhist scriptures that of the three mind-poisons – anger, attachment, and ignorance – ignorance is the most fundamental. If we can dispel our ignorance – our misunderstanding of the nature of reality – then all other mental negativities will fall away. Despite this, most of the time our ignorance is not something that directly hurts us. Working towards the uprooting of our ignorance is very good, but we need to see it as a long-term project. We cannot do it quickly or easily.

Attachment has a good side and a bad side. It is not always negative. Love and compassion are often associated with attachment, so there are good things that result from it. Its negative aspect is that while there is attachment there is aversion. Attachment and aversion are two sides of the same coin: the more attachment we have, the more fear we have. Therefore, skilfully reducing our attachment is a positive thing for us to do. Unfortunately, it is not an easy thing for us to do, because this way of reacting to things is very deep-seated in us human beings. Again this is something of a long-term project.

Unlike attachment, anger is always totally negative. There's nothing good about it. It burns us, and it burns others. Whoever it touches is harmed. It is the most directly harmful of the mind-poisons. However, because it has a flame-like nature, it is also the easiest to work on. The Buddha recommended that the first emotion we should work on is our anger. Once

we have learned how to deal with it, then we can turn our attention to deeper problems.

Of course, knowing how to work on our anger only benefits us if we want to work on it. That's why we need to reflect upon the uselessness of anger. We need to be clear in our own minds why working on our anger is beneficial to us. Only then can we begin.

Questioner: Rinpoche, I live with two friends in an apartment. And the problem is ... they don't clean the bathroom! I clean the bathroom three or four times before asking them if they would clean it. When I do ask them they say: "We have cleaned the bathroom! Have you cleaned the bathroom?!" I am afraid to ask them again, because they react so angrily. Anyway, earlier today I had an idea! It may be compassionate, I don't know. I wrote our names on a piece of paper and said: "Twice a week we must clean the bathroom and we must take it in turns. Every time one

of us cleans the bathroom, he must write the date on this piece of paper and sign it." What do you think?

Rinpoche: Good idea. Maybe it will work, maybe it won't work. If it doesn't work, then you have to choose either to live with your friends and a dirty bathroom, or move somewhere else with a clean bathroom but without your friends!

Questioner: You said that we should ask ourselves whether or not we can do something to make a bad situation better, but I often find this difficult to judge. Sometimes I think that it is possible when it isn't, and vice versa. Is there a good way to judge whether we are actually able to do something helpful or not?

Rinpoche: You cannot always be completely sure if you can do something to improve things, but if you think there is a possibility

then you can always try. If you decide that there is something you can do, there is no need to worry: just get on and do it. If you decide that there is nothing you can do, if you have tried everything you can think of, you have to apply the second formula: "I have tried, but there is nothing more I can do, so there is no use worrying about it."

Most of the time there are certain things we can do, because whatever situation we are in there is always something that is not entirely negative. If we can see that and take advantage of that, then there is a possibility that things can improve and what we thought was a hopeless situation may start to look a bit brighter. But it's very important to understand that life is not always a bed of roses. There will be problems. Life is about having problems and solving problems, isn't it? If we expect that once we've solved this problem then we will live happily ever afterwards, we are mistaken. That's not the way things are. It's not the case

that if my friends clean the bathroom, then all my problems will be solved. Maybe we will have a clean bathroom, but another problem will come along. Sometimes it may even be better to accept the fact that we do not have such a clean bathroom. If we expect that after we solve one problem everything is going to be 'tip-top', we are not being realistic. Everything is not going to be completely perfect, but I think we have to go with that. One has to be prepared to face problems and understand that life is about solving problems. We have to enjoy life while we are dealing with our problems, not put our enjoyment of life off until they are all solved.

Not everybody is like us. Different people need different things. Different people want different things. Not everybody will do exactly as we wish them to. If we expect everybody to do what we wish them to do, then we are heading for disappointment. We have to accept the fact that people have their

own ways: some good, some not so good, some that we like, and some that we don't like. I think a certain broadness of mind is very important. That's how we can become easier to live with. If we think everybody should be as we want them to be, or everything should be as we want it to be, and nothing less is good enough, then we will make life very difficult for others and difficult for ourselves as well. If, on the other hand, we accept that everybody has their own ways, their different abilities and different weaknesses, then we will find we have more breathing space. This broadness of mind is not a bad thing. It may mean learning to live with something that is not what we believe to be the absolute best, but it will bring better understanding between ourselves and others, and help us to be more relaxed and at peace, which is very important.

Questioner: Can you say a little more about fear, and how we can deal with fear?

Rinpoche: As I said earlier, facing it is the first and most important way to deal with fear, because when we really face our fears, generally they are not that terrible. It's the drama, the fear of the fear, which is the most terrifying thing: "It will be terrible! It will be terrible!" When the thing actually happens, or we really face it, generally it's not too bad.

The more we run away from the things we fear, the more afraid of those things we will become. We have to face them. If we have stage fright the best way to deal with it is to face the audience. If we are afraid of heights, we can begin by climbing to a slightly higher place and looking down. Of course, the first time we do this we may tremble, but slowly, slowly we get used to it and then we discover that it is not so terrible after all.

Complete freedom from fear comes from the complete understanding of our true nature. In Buddhism we try to investigate and analyse what our true nature really is. This enquiry

reveals that everything is transitory. Whether we like it or not, everything is constantly changing. Everything is interdependent and impermanent. There is no 'thing' in me or anywhere else which is separate or permanent. What we think of as our Self is actually a compounded phenomenon arising out of an infinite number of causes. When we understand deeply that there is nothing called a Self that we can or need to secure, we experience our true nature as clear consciousness, which cannot be changed or harmed by anything. When we see the way we truly are, a deep confidence arises that there is nothing we need to fear.

However, until we reach that stage it is important to have the courage to allow ourselves to have feelings of fear. We shouldn't shut off to them, or close down to them. We should let them come up.

The real objective of meditation is not to have good or fantastic experiences. If you

have a fantastic experience like becoming extremely blissful, or having a vision of an Enlightened Being, it's nice. But if you ask a real Master about it, generally they will tell you that it's neither really good nor bad, because like everything else it's transitory. If we feel very good now, it's okay, very nice, but that doesn't mean that we will feel good all the time. Maybe tomorrow we won't feel that good. Therefore, there's nothing that special about these experiences. Also, if we do have a fantastic experience there is a danger that we will try to cling to it, which will lead to disappointment, because like all experiences it passes. When it's gone we will try to get it back, and when we realize that we can't get it back, we will get even more upset.

The real purpose of meditation is to be able to let any kind of experience come and have no aversion to it. If we have an experience which is happy, joyful, and pleasant, then we enjoy it, but we don't treat it as anything more

than a transitory experience: we don't cling to it. Likewise, if we have an experience which is not nice – which causes fear, anger, or pain – we don't treat it as anything more than a transitory experience: we let it come, and we let it go.

Experiences are like the seasons – the winter comes and brings snow and ice; the spring comes and melts the snow and ice; the summer comes and brings sunshine and green leaves; the autumn comes, the sun fades and the leaves turn yellow; then again the winter comes.

We can't stop the seasons changing, but if we say: "Winter is coming, it's very, very bad!" we will cause ourselves suffering. If we have a lot of aversion to winter we will suffer throughout the whole of winter. That's no use, because we can't stop winter coming. If on the other hand we have a different attitude and say: "Winter is coming, so I will enjoy the winter!", then when the snow starts to fall it's very nice.

When we can let things come and let things go without aversion, then whatever experiences we go through we will be able to cope. When we react to experiences with a lot of aversion, we will suffer. We cannot run away from fear: fear is the wish to run away from something.

There is a story about a Tibetan man called Kee-huja who was travelling alone and at night through a place said to be haunted by evil spirits. He was very tired so he decided to set up his camp and get some sleep. During the night he was woken by a tiny, squeaky voice that seemed to be whispering his name: "Kee-huja." At first he wasn't sure if he was imagining it, so he sat up and listened carefully. Again he heard the tiny voice: "Keehuja." He was really frightened: "This must be the voice of an evil spirit!" he thought. Then he noticed some horsemen riding through the darkness towards him. Terrified, Kee-huja jumped onto his horse and rode as fast as he could. After

a while he decided to stop and listen for the voice. There it was again, still whispering his name: "Kee-huja." He looked back and saw that the horsemen were still riding through the darkness towards him, and they were gaining on him. Frantically he started riding again. He rode as hard and as fast as he could. After a while he decided to stop again, but the same thing happened. This continued for many hours, until, frightened out of his wits, Kee-huja rode all the way back to his home. When he got there he told everyone how he had been chased by ghosts. Once he had calmed down a bit, he decided to go to bed. But when he climbed into his bed he heard the tiny voice again: "Kee-huja." And he panicked: "Oh no! The evil spirit followed me all the way home!" Then he realised that the voice wasn't a voice at all, it was the sound of him breathing in and out through his nose.

Questioner: You suggested that fears become bigger when we run away from them, but sometimes running away is good for our survival. Isn't fear actually necessary for our survival? Isn't it a basic part of our survival instinct?

Rinpoche: Fear is not necessary for survival. Wisdom is necessary for survival. When I'm saying we should try to become less fearful, I'm not suggesting that we should become totally reckless, and start doing things without thinking about them first. But if fear is the only driving force behind our actions then they will become almost involuntary. We will feel forced to act in a particular way, regardless of whether it is negative or positive. And we will never feel at ease. Everything we do will be an emotional burden. If instead of acting through fear we simply act on the basis of what will produce a positive outcome, then we can act with joy.

Of course we have to do what is right and good and avoid doing what is not right and not good. If we put our hand in a fire it will get burned. We know that, and we know that we don't want to get burned, so we don't put our hand in a fire. If on the basis of facts we decide that we don't want to do something, because it's neither good for us or anyone else, then that's okay. That's not fear, that's wisdom. However, a lot of the time our fears are not based on facts, but on misapprehensions and mistaken assumptions. On many occasions we don't dare to do things because we are too afraid, only to discover later on that our fears were unfounded.

Our fear is so deep-seated and so basic to our reactions, not because we need it, but because its root cause is our absolutely fundamental misunderstanding, or ignorance, of the nature of reality. It is, therefore, very difficult for us to completely overcome all our fear, but the more we work on it the freer and more joyful we will become.

That doesn't make us any less fit for survival. It actually makes us more fit for survival. Most real dangers do not arise through being brave but through being panicky. It is said that in a dangerous situation like a house fire, most of the accidents happen when people panic. When we panic we do things which are harmful to ourselves and harmful to others. If we work to reduce our fear we will become stronger, our judgements will be more intelligent, and we will be better able to perform the actions that we need to.

We should not be reckless in a dangerous situation, but if we are too frightened we will freeze-up. When we were fleeing Tibet, some people froze when they were being shot at and they could not ride their horses. What you have to do then is kick them on the bottom! Then they will be able to move again. It's true. It happened many times.

In Kham, where I come from, there used to be lots of robbers and highwaymen. The

first thing they did before deciding whether or not to rob someone, was to see how easy it was to scare them. If they could scare them, then they robbed them. If they could not scare them, then they decided it was too dangerous and left them alone.

There was a band of robbers who lived on a trade route in a remote area of Kham. One day they saw a man coming along the road. He had a rifle, a pistol, a sword and a good horse. The robbers decided to come out of their hiding place and walk towards him: to see if he would be frightened. When the man saw them, he jumped off his horse, ran behind a rock and took out his rifle. Some of the robbers thought he must be a very dangerous person and that they should leave him alone. But then they noticed he had taken out his pistol as well, and they realised that he was scared. So the robbers went after him and robbed him of his rifle, his pistol, his sword, and his horse.

On another occasion, this band of robbers saw a different man riding along the road. He didn't have a rifle, or a pistol, or a sword. The robbers came out of their hiding place and tried to scare him. But he rode straight towards them. When he got to the group one of the robbers stepped forward and asked him if he had any snuff. The man replied: "Yes, you want some snuff?" The robber told him that he did. So the man pulled out a snuff box, took the robbers hand, and put some snuff into his palm. Then, whilst looking directly into the robber's eyes, he tightened his grip, until it almost made the robber cry. "Do you want anymore?" He asked the robber. Very politely the robber said: "No, thank you very much." Then the man rode off and nobody followed him.

If you are scared people are more likely to attack you. The same is true of animals. They are much more likely to attack you if you are scared of them. A horse breaker once told me

that the golden rule for taming a horse is not to be frightened. If you are not afraid, then you can do it, no problem. The moment you are frightened the horse will jump.

Questioner: It is said that the Green Tara practice can help us with our fear. My experience tells me that it works, but I don't understand how it works. Can you tell me?

Rinpoche: The main concept behind it is that although all the Great Bodhisattvas have made a vow to reach Enlightenment for the sake of all beings, they also dedicated their efforts to more specific aspirations. When Tara made her commitment to work for the benefit of all beings, she prayed: "All of the positive deeds that I do, may they give me the power to release beings from their fear. Anyone who remembers me, thinks of me, says my name, or prays to me, may they be blessed with fearlessness. And for the benefit of beings may I always be reborn

47

in a female form." Vajrasattva dedicated his efforts to the purification of negative deeds; Manjushri to revealing wisdom. They all made a special dedication.

As you know, in Buddhism we are always talking about interdependence. Tara might have the energy to give us fearlessness, but she can't do that by herself. If she could, then she would have already done it. It is the interdependence of our trust in her, our prayers to her, and her fearless energy that causes us to receive the blessing.

Questioner: I try to practise, and when I do I get a lot of joy out of it. But in my day-to-day life I often find myself being drawn away from my practice by more worldly things. I also suffer from laziness and forgetfulness. What should I do about this?

Rinpoche: I think re-inspiring ourselves again and again is very important. This is where the

sangha can play a valuable role. Being part of a community means we can find support and encouragement when we need it. When we feel inspired from interacting with nice people, hearing a good teaching, or reading a good book, we practise. It is not easy to maintain this sense of inspiration by ourselves, so it's very helpful to have a little bit of a sangha we can meet up with.

Of course, we can't be totally inspired everyday, but if we make our practice part of our daily routine then in spite of this we can still work on our habits. Buddhist practice is about working on our habits, so if we don't do it regularly we won't gain much benefit. Generally we should keep our practice fairly simple, just do one or two things. How much time we spend doing them depends on our other commitments, but practising regularly is very important.

When I need to be re-inspired, I read the Songs of Milarepa: they're very inspiring in

the original Tibetan. Reading or listening to a nice teaching can definitely help us when we are feeling down and uninspired. At first we might think: "Oh I know all this, I've heard it all before." But if we keep listening, every so often something will make our ears prick up. If we listen to a teaching now, then listen to it again in a year, somehow it will be different. We will hear new things and find a new way of understanding the teaching.

Thank you all very much.

All my babbling,
In the name of Dharma
Has been set down faithfully
By my dear students of pure vision.

I pray that at least a fraction of the wisdom
Of those enlightened teachers
Who tirelessly trained me
Shines through this mass of incoherence.

May the sincere efforts of all those
Who have worked tirelessly
Result in spreading the true meaning of Dharma
To all who are inspired to know.

May this help dispel the darkness of ignorance
In the minds of all living beings
And lead them to complete realisation
Free from all fear.

Ringu Tulku

In memory of Marion Knight
who passed away before
this book went to print.

Acknowledgements

We wish to thank the original team that produced the first edition of this book; Brigit Habetz, for her transcription work; Margaret Ford, for her support and advice with editing; Jude Tarrant, for design and layout; Andy Powers, for his drawings; Alison de Ledesma, for distribution; and Cait Collins, for all the work she put into establishing the Lazy Lama series.

For this second edition we would like to thank; Paul O'Connor, for this new layout, design and cover image; Dr Dirk de Klerk, for the cover photo; Dr Conrad Harvey & Rebecca O'Connor, for the new Lazy Lama logo illustration; Marion Knight and Annie Dibble, for proof reading.

About the Author

Ringu Tulku Rinpoche is a Tibetan Buddhist Master of the Kagyu Order. He was trained in all schools of Tibetan Buddhism under many great masters including HH the 16th Gyalwang Karmapa and HH Dilgo Khyentse Rinpoche. He took his formal education at Namgyal Institute of Tibetology, Sikkim and Sampurnananda Sanskrit University, Varanasi, India. He served as Tibetan Textbook Writer and Professor of Tibetan Studies in Sikkim for 25 years.

Since 1990, he has been travelling and teaching Buddhism and meditation in Europe, America, Canada, Australia and Asia. He participates in various interfaith and 'Science and Buddhism' dialogues and is the author of several books on Buddhist topics. These include Path to Buddhahood, Daring Steps,

The Ri-me Philosophy of Jamgon Kongtrul the Great, Confusion Arises as Wisdom, the Lazy Lama series and the Heart Wisdom series, as well as several children's books, available in Tibetan and European languages.

He founded the organisations:
Bodhicharya - see www.bodhicharya.org
and Rigul Trust - see www.rigultrust.org.

Other books by Bodhicharya Publications

The Lazy Lama Series:

No. 1 - Buddhist Meditation
No. 2 - The Four Noble Truths
No. 3 - Refuge: Finding a Purpose and a Path
No. 4 - Bodhichitta: Awakening Compassion and Wisdom
No. 5 - Living without Fear and Anger

Heart Wisdom Series:

No. 1 - Mahamudra & Dzogchen: *[reprinted in Heart Wisdom No. 4]*
No. 2 - The Ngöndro: *Foundation Practices of Mahamudra*
No. 3 - From Milk to Yoghurt: *A Recipe for Living and Dying*
No. 4 - Like Dreams and Clouds:
    Emptiness and Interdependence; Mahamudra and Dzogchen
No. 5 - Dealing with Emotions: *Scattering the Clouds*
No. 6 - The Journey from Head to Heart: *Along a Buddhist Path*

See: www.bodhicharya.org/publications

Rigul TrusT

Patron: Ringu Tulku Rinpoche

Rigul Trust is a UK charity whose objectives are the relief of poverty and financial hardship, the advancement of education, the advancement of religion, the relief of sickness, the preservation of good health.

Our main project is helping with health and education in Rigul, Tibet, the homeland of Ringu Tulku Rinpoche where his monastery is. We currently fund Dr Chuga, the nurse, the doctor's assistant, the running costs of the health clinic, the teachers, the cooks and the children's education plus two, free, hot meals a day at school.

We also help raise funds for disasters like earthquakes, floods, and help with schools in India and other health and welfare projects. All administration costs are met privately by volunteers.

100%

OF ALL DONATIONS GOES TO FUND HEALTH, EDUCATION AND POVERTY RELIEF PROJECTS

Rigul Trust

13 St. Francis Avenue, Southampton, SO18 5QL U.K.

info@rigultrust.org

UK Charity Registration No: 1124076

For an up to date list of books by Ringu Tulku,
please see the Books section at

www.bodhicharya.org

*All proceeds received by Bodhicharya Publications from
the sale of this book go direct to humanitarian and
educational projects because the work involved
in producing this book has been given free of charge.*